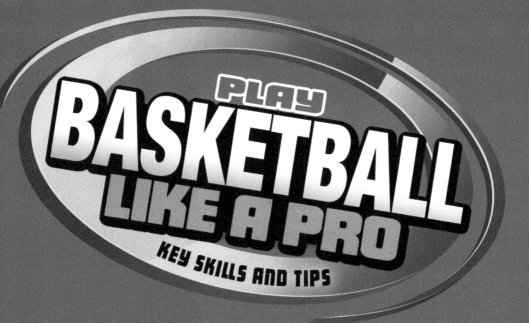

PLAY BASKETBALL LIKE A PRO

KEY SKILLS AND TIPS

BY NATE LEBOUTILLIER

Consultant:
Jeffrey L. Chambers
Head Athletic Trainer
Minnesota State University
Mankato, Minnesota

CAPSTONE PRESS
a capstone imprint

Sports Illustrated KIDS Play Like the Pros is published by Capstone Press,
1710 Roe Crest Drive, North Mankato, Minnesota 56003
www.capstonepub.com

Library of Congress Cataloging-in-Publication Data
LeBoutillier, Nate.
    Play basketball like a pro : key skills and tips / By Nate LeBoutillier.
    p. cm.—(Sports illustrated kids : play like the pros)
    Includes bibliographical references and index.
    Summary: "Provides instructional tips on how to improve one's
basketball skills, including quotes and advice from professional coaches
and athletes"—Provided by publisher.
    ISBN 978-1-4296-4826-4 (library binding)
    ISBN 978-1-4296-5645-0 (paperback)
    ISBN 978-1-4765-0160-4 (e-book)
1. Basketball—Training—Juvenile literature. I. Title. II. Series.
GV885.1.L43 2011
796.323—dc22   2010007242

EDITORIAL CREDITS

Aaron Sautter and Anthony Wacholtz, editors; Ted Williams, designer;
    Eric Gohl, media researcher; Laura Manthe, production specialist

PHOTO CREDITS

Shutterstock/Carlos Caetano, cover, 3 (basketball); kentoh, design element;
    Vjom, design element
Sports Illustrated/Al Tielemans, 14, 25 (bottom); Bill Frakes, cover (right),
    13, 27; Bob Rosato, 16, 19 (bottom); Damian Strohmeyer, 11 (top),
    19 (top), 29; David E. Klutho, 23 (top), 25 (top), 26; John Biever,
    17 (top), 24, 28; John W. McDonough, cover (left), 4-5, 7 (top), 8, 9
    (all), 10, 11 (bottom), 12, 15, 17 (bottom), 18, 20, 21, 22, 23 (bottom);
    Manny Millan, 7 (bottom); Peter Read Miller, 6

TABLE OF CONTENTS

TIPS ▼

▼ FEATURES

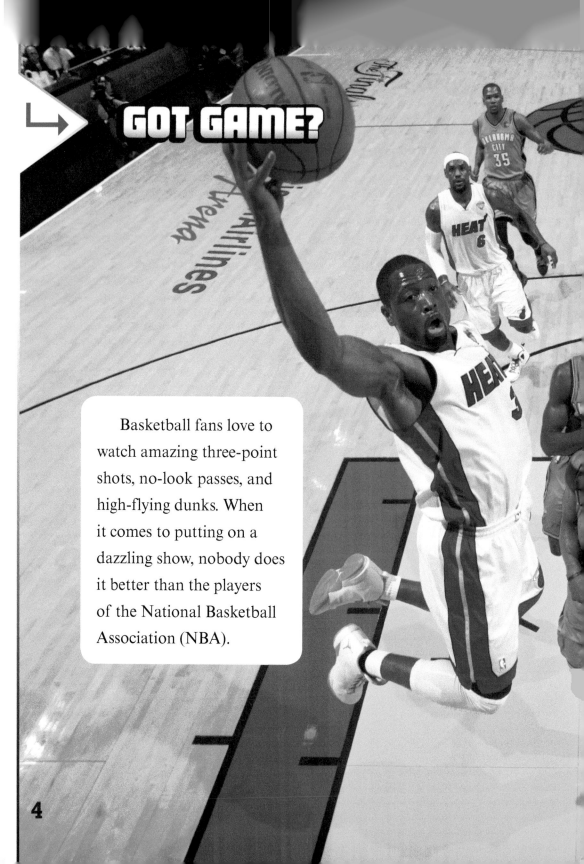

GOT GAME?

Basketball fans love to watch amazing three-point shots, no-look passes, and high-flying dunks. When it comes to putting on a dazzling show, nobody does it better than the players of the National Basketball Association (NBA).

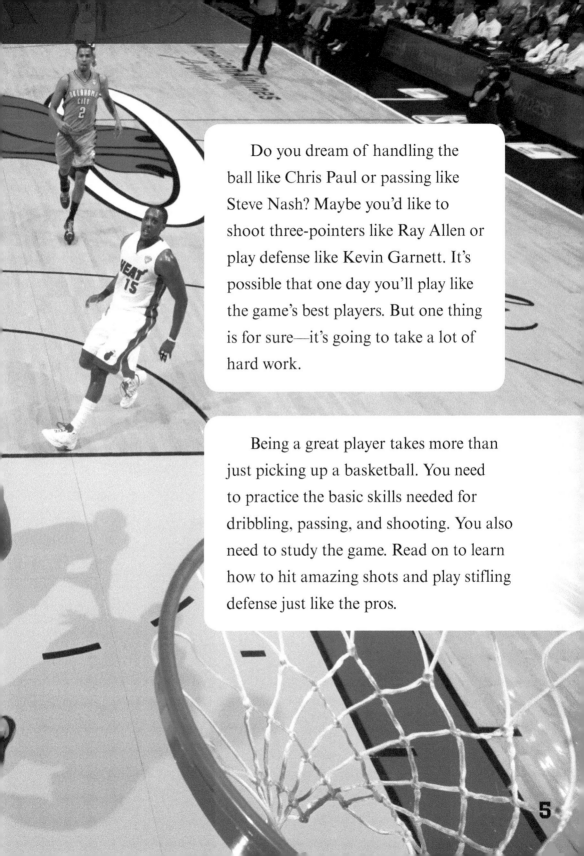

Do you dream of handling the ball like Chris Paul or passing like Steve Nash? Maybe you'd like to shoot three-pointers like Ray Allen or play defense like Kevin Garnett. It's possible that one day you'll play like the game's best players. But one thing is for sure—it's going to take a lot of hard work.

Being a great player takes more than just picking up a basketball. You need to practice the basic skills needed for dribbling, passing, and shooting. You also need to study the game. Read on to learn how to hit amazing shots and play stifling defense just like the pros.

The best players are in great basketball shape. This is different than simply being "in shape." Basketball is a game of quick starts and fast sprints. Players need to constantly shuffle, jump, and aim throughout the game. Follow these drills to get into tip-top basketball shape.

LADDER SPRINTS

Start on one baseline. Sprint to the nearest free-throw line, touch it, and then sprint back to the baseline. Next, sprint in the same way to half court and back. Then run to the opposite free-throw line and back. Finally, sprint to the opposite baseline and back. If you can finish in about 35 seconds, you're doing great. Take a short break, then do another set.

↳ baseline—the out of bounds lines at each end of the court

BALL SPRINTS

Being able to run with the ball is a key part of the game. Practice running ladder sprints while dribbling the ball. If you can run fast while dribbling, you'll have a better chance of outpacing your opponents.

BOX JUMPS

Find or make three wooden boxes of different heights. The boxes should be about as high as your calf, knee, and thigh. Jump on top of the boxes one at a time. Practice increasing your speed between jumps. You'll be jumping higher for those big shots in no time.

Michael Jordan was possibly the most talented basketball player in history. But talent only took him so far. Jordan wanted to get an edge over other NBA players. In 1989, he started working out with personal trainer Tim Grover. "He said he'd try it out for a month, and it ended up being 15 years," said Grover. Jordan's intense training helped him lead the Chicago Bulls to six NBA championships in the 1990s.

Michael Jordan's Secret to Success

2 HOW TO DRIBBLE

Dribbling the basketball is an essential skill. You need to be able to dribble at full speed through traffic. Be sure to practice these tips with both hands so you feel comfortable dribbling with either one.

FINGERTIP CONTROL

Accurate dribbling is done with your fingertips, not your palms. Your palm shouldn't slap the ball when you dribble. Instead, cup your hand upside down. Keeping the ball on your fingertips will give you better control.

KEEP IT LOW

To keep defensive players from stealing the ball, keep it low. A low dribble also lets you change direction more quickly. You don't have to wait long for the ball to bounce back before cutting left or right.

STAY ALERT

It's important to keep your head up while dribbling. Be sure to watch the defense, the basket, and your teammates. By staying aware, you'll be ready to make a move when you see an opening.

"I learned at a young age to dribble with both hands, and that allowed me to be more creative when I'd go against bigger and stronger opponents."
-STEVE NASH, POINT GUARD, PHOENIX SUNS

The closest shots to the rim aren't always the easiest. Layups take good **coordination** that involves aiming and shooting while on the move. Try these moves for greater accuracy on the run.

PERFECT THE TAKE OFF

The trickiest part of a layup is perfecting the footwork. For a right-handed layup, raise your right knee and jump with your left foot. As you approach the basket, reach the ball toward it with your right hand. For a left-handed layup, take off with your right foot and shoot with your left hand.

USE THE GLASS

Layups are done while moving at full speed. But if you force the ball too hard it might bounce off the rim.

To take some of the force off the ball, use the backboard. Aim for the square, and the ball should bank into the hoop. Be sure to use a light touch.

REVERSE LAYUPS

When defenders are pressuring you, try using a reverse layup. Dribble the ball a couple steps farther than in a normal layup. Begin your jump while under the hoop. Then flip the ball behind you to bounce it off the backboard and into the hoop. The reverse layup helps block the defender from getting at the ball.

HOW TO SHOOT FREE THROWS

It's the game's simplest yet most nerve-racking shot. Free throws only count for one point each. But they add up and can mean the difference between winning and losing a game. Work on these steps to build confidence at the stripe.

GET INTO POSITION

Line up your toes behind the free-throw line. Your feet should be about shoulder-width apart. Support the ball with your non-shooting hand. Keep your shooting hand across the ball's seams. The forearm of your shooting hand should be kept straight and facing the basket. Before shooting, bend your knees. The power in a free throw comes from your legs, not your arms.

TAKE YOUR SHOT

Be sure to aim for a spot just above the rim. As you take the shot, straighten your legs and shooting arm. Be sure to **follow through** with your wrist. For a good follow through, pretend to reach for the rim with your shooting hand.

Rick Barry was one of the greatest free-throw shooters in NBA history. His underhand, or "granny style," free-throw shots were unique. The style was popular in the early days of basketball. But over time, players stopped using it. Barry was one of the last to use it in the 1970s. "Underhand is a totally natural, relaxed position," said Barry. " ... I never had to worry about being tight and tired. The more I practiced [underhand], the more confidence I got and the better I felt with it." During his career, Barry made an impressive 89 percent of his free throws.

Granny Style

Three-point shots take coordination, timing, and accuracy to pull off. If done right, the result is a beautiful net-swishing three points. Shoot for perfection with these tips.

PERFECT YOUR FORM

Set your feet shoulder-width apart. This **stance** is important for proper balance and aim. Keep your shooting hand behind the ball and your wrist in a cocked position. Use your other hand to keep the ball steady.

SHOOT IT

Bend your knees and then jump as high as possible. Hold your head steady. Release the ball at the highest point of your jump to avoid having your shot blocked. Snap your shooting wrist on the release, and be sure to follow through.

EYES ON THE GOAL

When making your shot, always keep your eye on the basket. Some players look at the rim. Some look at the backboard. Find a spot that works best for you. Keep practicing until you can sink the ball from any point on the three-point arc.

"I never looked at the consequences of missing a big shot. When you think about the consequences, you always think of a negative result."
-MICHAEL JORDAN, FORMER SHOOTING GUARD, CHICAGO BULLS

HOW TO MAKE INTERIOR MOVES

A powerful inside game is important for any offense. Getting close shots around the basket helps put points on the board. Practice these moves near the basket, and it could lead to slam-dunk success.

TURNAROUND JUMPER

One easy interior shot is done by simply turning around to shoot the ball. Practice the turnaround jumper by using either foot as a **pivot** point. Spin in either direction to face the basket, then jump off with the other foot. The spin move should help you get a clean shot past the defender.

A great move to use with the turnaround jumper is the up and under. Once you have the ball, pivot on your foot to fake a turnaround jumper. When your opponent tries to block the shot, pivot back again. This move can help you sneak around the defender for a simple layup.

HOOK IT

The hook shot is a classic basketball move. If done correctly, the hook is nearly unblockable. Start close to the basket. Jump up and sweep the ball behind your head with your shooting arm. Release the ball at your hand's highest point and let it drop through the hoop.

HOW TO MAKE PERIMETER MOVES

Sometimes the defense tightens up and makes it hard to shoot from the perimeter. In this case, you need to try to move to the inside, or at least fake doing so. Shimmy and shake with these perimeter moves to get yourself free from the defender.

CROSSOVER

Sometimes a quick change of direction can shake off a defender. While dribbling right, plant your right foot and quickly dribble the ball over to your left hand. Keep moving toward the hoop for a quick jump shot or a dazzling layup.

JAB STEP

The jab step is a useful move to separate yourself from the defender. Jab your foot forward like you are going to drive to the hoop. If your opponent backs off, immediately step back and fire off a jump shot. If your opponent stays close, fake your shot instead, then dribble past the defender.

PICK AND ROLL

This standard two-person play helps knock defenders off the ball carrier. Watch for your teammate to set a pick, or screen. Then bolt in that direction with a quick dribble. Run close by your teammate to lose your defender. Your teammate should then pivot

and roll toward the basket. If he's open, quickly pass to him so he can take a shot. But if you have a clear lane, take it to the rim for two points.

↳ perimeter—the area surrounding the three-point line

↳ screen—a play in which a player gets between a defender and a teammate

19

HOW TO REBOUND

Rebounding is a key skill for both offense and defense. The best rebounders are hard-working hustlers. They aren't afraid to do a little pushing and shoving to get the ball. Work on these pointers to crash the boards.

BOX OUT

When a shot goes up, get close to your opponent. Using your rear, pivot into him and keep him at your back. Jut your elbows out to keep him there. Make sure to stay between your opponent and the hoop.

KNOW THE SPOT

The key to rebounding is knowing where to be if a shot misses. For long shots, rebounds will usually bounce farther out from the hoop. If a shot misses from the baseline, the ball usually bounces to the opposite side of the court. When the opponent shoots, always assume it will miss and hustle into the correct position.

TIP OR TAP

One challenge in rebounding is that many players are going for the ball. If you're not sure you can get it, try to tip or tap the ball to yourself or to a teammate. You can even use the backboard to help get hold of it.

"If you want to become a great rebounder, it's about will and hard work. I know if I'm rebounding and we're dominating the boards, we're going to win the game."
-DWIGHT HOWARD, CENTER, ORLANDO MAGIC

HOW TO PASS

Giving can be better than receiving on the basketball court. The best passers know how to get the ball to an open teammate. Try these passing tips to hit your teammate for the score.

CHEST PASS

With both hands, bring the ball close to your chest with your elbows out. Step forward with one foot and push the ball out from your chest. At the release, both of your thumbs should be pointed toward the floor. This creates some backspin on the ball, which makes it easier for your teammate to catch it.

OVERHEAD PASS

Use the overhead pass for long-distance passing. Hold the ball with both hands. Swing your arms over your head and snap them forward to release the ball. Be sure to step into the throw. Your legs power the pass as much as your arms.

BOUNCE PASS

Bounce passes are good for getting the ball past a defender. Aim for a spot on the floor midway between you and your teammate. Be sure to throw the ball hard enough to get it to your teammate. Give the ball some backspin so it doesn't skid along the floor. Skidding makes the ball difficult to catch and easier for a defender to steal it.

NO-LOOK PASS

In a no-look pass, you send the ball to an open teammate while looking in a different direction. Don't look directly at your teammates. Watch for them out of the corners of your eyes. When you know where they will be, look away from them as you pass. The defender will often move toward where you're looking instead of where the ball is going.

10 HOW TO RUN FAST BREAKS

Fast breaks happen when there are more offensive players than defensive players near the basket. Teams that are good at the fast break have a good chance of winning the game. Practice these tips until fast breaks become a natural part of your game.

GET AN EARLY START

Fast breaks start with extra hustle. After a missed shot, be sure your team grabs the defensive rebound. Then sprint to the other end of the court ahead of the other team.

THROW THE OUTLET PASS

If you have the ball, look for an open teammate. Throw the ball one-handed like a baseball or football. The outlet pass isn't as accurate as a two-handed pass, but it is much faster. Your team should be able to take an open shot ahead of the other team.

FINISH IT

If you receive the ball on a fast break, get to the middle of the court. You'll see the court and the players in front of you better from that position. Scan the court for an opening. If you have an open shot, go for it. Or look for an open teammate who can take the shot.

Fans often overlook defense, but it's an important part of the game. Great defenders are feisty, tireless, and resourceful. Regardless of skill, most players can improve their defense through practice. Try these moves to step up your defensive play.

DEFENSIVE SHUFFLE

Get into a stance with your knees bent. Extend your arms out from your sides, and keep your eyes up. Whichever way your opponent moves, shuffle in that direction. Don't overlap your feet as you shuffle. To avoid getting faked-out, watch your opponent's midsection instead of his eyes. Always try to stay between your opponent and the basket.

DENY THE PASS

To deny the pass, try to stay between the player you're guarding and the ball. Keep an eye on both the ball and your opponent. You want to be ready to step in to block the pass or steal the ball.

TALK, TALK, TALK

Playing effectively on offense takes an entire team. The same is true for defense. When you're on the court, talk to your teammates. Better yet, yell. Let them know if you see a pick coming, or if they should switch people to guard. You can never talk too much on defense.

"I understand how defense works. Communication's probably the biggest thing when it comes to defense."
-KEVIN GARNETT, FORWARD, BOSTON CELTICS

12 USING TEAMWORK

You can be the greatest basketball player of all time, but basketball is still a team game. The best teams have players that know how to work together. They sacrifice for each other and bring out each other's best efforts. Work on these tips to become a team player.

TALK AND LISTEN

Communication can help win basketball games. Keep talking to make sure everyone is running the same play. And of course, listen to your coaches. They can help you become the best player you can be.

DON'T BE SELFISH

Don't worry about being in the spotlight. When you're in the game, pass the ball to your teammates. Help guard the hoop if a teammate gets beat on defense. You need to trust that your teammates will help out when you make mistakes too.

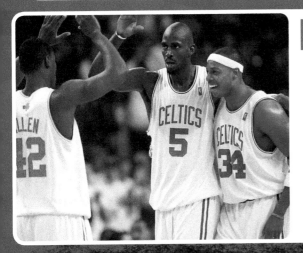

BE POSITIVE

Everyone makes mistakes at some point. If teammates make mistakes, be encouraging. They'll often be able to make up for it with good plays later in the game.

"I'll do whatever it takes to win games, whether it's ... handing a cup of water to a teammate, or hitting the game-winning shot."
-KOBE BRYANT, GUARD, LOS ANGELES LAKERS

The tips in this book are just a starting point. Many people want to play like LeBron James or Dwyane Wade. But even the biggest stars had to start with the basics. With hard work and plenty of practice, one day you may be playing just like the pros.

GLOSSARY

BASELINE—the out-of-bounds line at each end of the court under the baskets

COORDINATION—the ability to control one's arms and legs to make them work together

FAST BREAK—a play in which a team gets a rebound, then sprints to the other end of the court to make a shot before the opposing team can stop them

FOLLOW THROUGH—to continue the shooting motion after the ball has been thrown

PERIMETER—the area around the three-point line on the court

PIVOT—to turn on a central point

REBOUND—to take possession of the ball after a missed shot

SCREEN—a play in which a player gets between a defender and a teammate; screens are also called picks

STANCE—the position of a player's feet and body

READ MORE

Burns, Brian, and Mark Dunning. *Skills in Motion: Basketball Step-by-Step.* New York: Rosen Central, 2010.

Gifford, Clive. *Basketball.* Personal Best. New York: PowerKids Press, 2009.

Robinson, Tom. *Basketball Skills.* How to Play Like a Pro. Berkeley Heights, N.J.: Enslow Elementary, 2009.

INTERNET SITES

FactHound offers a safe, fun way to find Internet sites related to this book. All of the sites on FactHound have been researched by our staff.

Here's all you do:

Visit *www.facthound.com*

Type in this code: 9781429648264

INDEX ⌐